LOOSE LIPPED SECRETS AND TWINKLING LIGHTS

Christopher Michael Carter

Supposed Crimes LLC • Matthews, North Carolina

All Rights Reserved
Copyright © 2019 Christopher Michael Carter

Published in the United States.

ISBN: 978-1-944591-65-6

www.supposedcrimes.com

This book is typeset in Goudy Old Style.

Dedicated to my father Ernest Lee Carter (1955-2018).

We miss you, Old Man.

More by Christopher Michael Carter

Poetry

Gun Control for Polar Bears
Reflections at Various Speeds

Fiction

Last Rights of the Capacitance
Blue Sweep
Agent Phoenix

Collections

Sharp Items & Bad Intentions
Beyond the Wall
Duo de Macabre
How to Sell Sunblock to a Vampire

Plays

Doomsday Think Tank

Table of Contents

The Process	9
Roses	13
Worth	14
Dreaming For Both of Us	15
The Fracture	16
Between Us	17
A Better Son	18
Carrier	19
Love Control	20
A Much Needed Lie	21
Unnoticed	22
Man of Promise	23
Waiting	24
Deadlines	25
The Animals	26
Repentant	28
Laughing Alone	29
Shades of You I	30
The Night Shore	33
Chosen	34
Challenge Accepted	36
2.0	37
Hungry Friends	38
Just the Way You Are	39
Erotic Strangers	40
Rain Dance	41
Masculine Love	42

Shades of You II	43
Lost Room	46
This is The End	47
A Sad Truth	48
Icy Home	49
An Affordable Life	50
A Visitor	51
Lost Time	52
Derailed	53
Voiceless	54
Bugs	55
Always Tomorrow	57
A Choice	58
Destination	59
My Poor Back	60
Drive	61
Shades of You III	62
Haunting	65
Powerless	66
When I'm Gone	67
Dead Battery	68
The Best of Us	69
Muse	70
Delivery of the Stars	71
Free Form	72
Holding On and Letting Go	73
REM Nightmares	74
This Writer Will Self-Destruct	75
Land First, Jump Second	76

To Whom It May Concern	77
Growth	78
The Company We Keep	79
Together Tomorrow	80
An Appointment in the Outer Realm	81
Bitter and Sour	82
A Reflection	83
These Hands	84
I Am the Darkness	86
Here We Are	87
She Doesn't...	89
The Humanity Special	92
An Alien in America	96
Do You	98
A Feast	99
Short Honeymoon	100
Decisions, Decisions	101
The Front Page	102
The Reptile Bar	103
The Dawn Limited	104
Abused	105
Bald Earth	106
Keep Searching	107
Old and Gray	108
Distract Me	110
Timid Termite	111
Fast and Slow	112
Apocalypse Morning	113
From the Soil to the Stars	115

Just One More	116
This is Our Home	117
I Just Want to Say...	125
About the Author	127

The Process

The curser blinks on an otherwise blank screen
The white stares back at me
My mind plays the possibilities
The characters deliver their lines
And move to their respective spots
My fingers move across the keys
Playing stenographer in a room full of people I've created
A line is flubbed
The current situation has taken a left turn
And is now off the rails
My fingers stop and I get out of my director's chair
I pull them back to where it went south
And offer new directions
New possibilities
I wait to see how it unfolds
The curser awaits
The blank white yearns to be filled
While I look like a crazy person staring at the screen with apparent blank eyes
The action unfolds
It gets good
My fingers try to keep up
It's working, it's really working
I stop to assess the situation
Characters pause on a cliffhanger
And look to me for what happens next
The writer's room in my head is alive
Pitches and suggestions are thrown out
Some fall flat, some stick
My fingers are like my characters
Waiting for the right moment
The ideas align like cogs in a wheel

It continues and words flow forth
My characters talk
My fingers fly
My mind edits
Delete delete delete
Pull it back
Begin again
No time for the curser to pulse
Pushing imaginary people to their limits
And I've reached mine
All avenues have been exhausted
Pride and happiness swells
Until
I read over everything
And hate every word
They've all deceived me
My hands, my characters
The writer's room as a whole
And I walk away
I carry on with the standard actions of a mundane day
But all the while my brain works
The writers scramble to meet their quota
To crack the code and fix the problem
Nothing comes
I want to scrap it all and start over
The writers and characters plead with me
Sleep on it, they say
I do what I'm supposed to, say what I'm supposed to say
But inside I struggle
While my body lives on autopilot
My mind works hard on a puzzle box with infinite sides
And just before I drift off to sleep
It comes to me - the answer
A choice to make

Get up and rush to get it down
Or try to infuse my dreams
When I next look at the scattered black over the white page
My hatred is gone
And I'm in love again
The routine starts all over
Love passion hatred love
The work
Mental strains, tired fingers and tired eyes
A restless spirit until completion
When flesh is put on the skeleton
I work to put a layer of skin on my creation
Before I dissect it
I surgically take out malignant parts
And remove blockage
The writer's room fights over what's benign and what's not
The work is constructed and reconstructed
The tired strain stays
Nothing looks familiar
A mess of notes and random conversations between make believe people
I walk away again but it never leaves me
Never leaves my mind
I look upon it with fresh eyes
It doesn't resemble what it was
I'm torn on whether or not I love what it's become
Or hate that it's defied my initial direction
The curser blinks steadily
My fingers caress the keys awaiting to strike
The end
Finished
Time to dissect again
Reshape, remold
Its change only recognizable to me

Only time will tell what comes out of this
And then tomorrow I'll start all over
A new blank page
Waiting to be filled

Roses

Roses grow in her footprints
Their thorns are as sharp as their beauty
She steps lightly in frolicking springs
Her feet press into the earth
Her toes curl and grasp the ground briefly
And release
Step after step is taken
Seeds planted
And then they sprout
And soon they bloom
She dances everywhere
Leaving roses in her wake
Stems of razor sharp thorns intertwine
Trails erupt in vibrant red
Over the hills
And through the town
Roses sprout up through the streets
Breaking concrete and pavement
The city is filled with the flowers
They disrupt traffic
She's asked to leave
And so she does
Oh how they'll miss the beauty she brought
But she'll be back
She always comes back

Worth

I am nothing
I am worthless
I am reminded of this
Every day
I don't try hard enough
I don't communicate
I don't need a reminder of these
My faults
I need to get organized
I need to put in the effort
I need to remember
To change
My apologies aren't welcome
My action is required
My chance to prove myself
Is now

Dreaming For Both of Us

You've all abandoned me
And now
I'm left to dream alone
My words needed to be read
But you left them to rot
I picked up the letters
Scattered and alone
And made you something new
But you didn't care
Regardless of your lack of faith in me
I keep building and building
You may come back around some day
You may not
But I'm still here
Dreaming enough for both of us

The Fracture

Mommy and daddy are done
A big adjustment
The kids wonder what will happen to them
Wonder what happened
If they're at fault
The parents assure them
But the doubt stays
And they grow up wondering
What they could've done differently
But they couldn't understand
It had run its course
And it's time to end it
They'll understand one day
When they're older
Until that day
The fracture stays

Between Us

We're broken
You and I
We don't speak on it
We don't divulge
But we know it
We stand together
Silently
Sharing looks that only we understand
The cracks spread
And we don't say a word
But we know it
Our smiles and jokes hide our truth
And our eyes hide our hearts
We share this
The bruises, the hurt
The loss, the loneliness
It's ours
And we walk
Hand in hand
Keeping it to ourselves

A Better Son

You left us too soon
I wasn't ready
Didn't make use of the time we had
Oh please turn back the hands
So I can hear your voice again
So I can tell you everything you missed
Your voice is fading
My ears reach for your last words
Like a drowning man reaches for the surface
Losing you was like losing a limb
I'd forgotten how to function
How to live
I haven't used this time wisely either
I should be working on myself
But I keep seeing you when I go to sleep
I need to know you're okay
I need you to talk to me
To listen to me
To tell me you left without worry
Without pain
I miss you
More than you'll ever know
I'm so sorry
For the time I wasted
For not reaching out
For not being present
For not being a better son
I'm trying now
But I know it's too late

CARRIER

In the dead of night
She told me her fantasies
Loose lipped secrets
And twinkling lights
All I remember was her breath in my ear
And her eyes in mine
The quiet stars above
She emptied herself
And I was full
Taking in every syllable
Her heart had wrenched out
She gave her all to me
And I accepted
When the last word escaped her lips
She vanished in the night
I still carry her with me

Love Control

She loves her
He loves him
But offense is taken
Society seems to hate love
They turn their noses up
And bite their thumbs
At love
The thing that binds us all together
Is shunned by the masses
Control
They want to control
Who we love
What love is
And how we express it
Love hard
And show them
Let our hearts beat
In defiance

A Much Needed Lie

Lie to me
In your sultry voice
Tell me things
I yearn to hear
Lie to me
In your beautiful tone
Tell me I'm your one
That I'm who you think about
When the sun goes down
And the moon rises
Lie to me
Tell me you love me
And that you'd die for me
As I would for you
Lie to me
Because I'd rather have that
Than your deafening silence

Unnoticed

I pour my heart out
But you won't listen
I bare my soul
But you don't notice
I work my fingers to the bone
But you don't see the growth
I give you my all
But you don't want me
Am I not doing enough for you?
I'm bleeding myself dry
Are my words really so inconsequential?
I'm begging you
But you won't read
I fear
Like me
My words will die
Unnoticed

Man of Promise

Please don't leave me
I don't know what I'd do without you
I live for you
Love for you
I know I'm a man of mistakes
A man of fault
But know that I am not my mistakes
Know also that I am a man of promise
And that promise shall be kept
Just don't give up on me

Waiting

He died
They cried
His life was over
They tried to live
His light went out
Theirs went dim
He was finally free
They missed him terribly
He was with his family now
But they were selfish and wanted him back
They wait
And wait
But he'll never return

Deadlines

Deadlines
Deadlines
Self-imposed deadlines
I'm slowly going insane
Quicker as the time draws near
Somebody help me
Please
Take some of this load off of me
I'm reaching out
I'm crying out
A still silence is the answer
I need to go it alone
While I still have me to count on

The Animals

Where are we
On the food chain
We keep animals in cages
And people in boxes
We give ourselves free reign
While handing out limitations
The food we eat
Must pass societal inspection
The current diet craze online
The ones we love
Must pass government code
Only legal affection required
The things we fight for
Are only allotted
We win what we're allowed
And lose what was rightfully ours
We complain
And call it fighting back
We're stepped on daily
But we're so used to the pressure
We call it life
How did we get here
We live like paupers
But are still royalty compared to others
Kings and Queens
Of our own boxes
We sentence others
While serving, ourselves
We preach love and equality
But act on hatred and fear
Build walls, burn bridges

High talk, low action
Why the animals have not taken over
I have no idea
Perhaps they're complacent too

Repentant

I'm ashamed
Ashamed of my actions
And ashamed of my inactions
My choices
My tone
My chosen words
I'm better than this
I know I am
I want to change
Want to start over
A clean slate
Is all I ask for
I'll put in the work
Put in the time
Just know that this is not the best me
What you've seen
Is a man amidst a struggle
A man broken down by life
A man who's willing
To shed his old skin
For new armor
I know you're ashamed too
You thought you knew me
Thought I was different
Didn't think I could behave in such a manner
Know that I'm truly sorry
I only hope that you can forgive me
And perhaps maybe someday
Start anew

Laughing Alone

Another day. Same life. Another car ride.
She said, "You're not the funny guy you used to be."
"What do you mean?" I asked.
"You used to be hilarious! You used to laugh all the time!"
"Eh, that guy's gone."
"No, I just think you're holding out on me."
"Nah, he's dead. The joke's over."
We continued the car ride in silence.
The laughter eventually stops when you're laughing alone.

SHADES OF YOU I

You work hard with no results
You know that something will come
But it's hard to explain that to everyone else
You don't have as many supporters as you do Facebook friends
You fear you'll never be as big as you should be
You love your friends and family
But feel it's hard to stay close
Friendships are a strange tightrope
The way you include others isn't the norm
You step on toes when you try to give them room
You want your friends as your family
You love them
But you don't feel the same in reply
You feel that art is life
And life is art
But it seems that very few share your beliefs
You often feel you're surrounded by wolves
You're a wolf as well
But you don't feel the same
Your surroundings appear feral
While you keep your composure
You've spent your life in the audience
And want one shot at having the podium to yourself
You want an audience
You want to be heard as you have heard others
You know your past
And can't change it
You know where your future lies
But it's hard to convince others
You're confused about your present
With great things ahead how can you be so unhappy?

You'll never know
You're surrounded but you're alone simultaneously
You're lonely
The loneliest person you know
You used to have to surround yourself with people
Then you wanted everyone gone
Now you're wishing everyone back
You're fickle
Lonely and fickle
Unsatisfied in your personal life
But happy to be in your profession
You miss everyone, even when you're with them
You live a life of regret
Everyone has 'the one that got away'
You have more than one that you missed out on
You're the King of the Ones that got away
And they'll never know
You married the one that almost got away
Learning from your mistakes
You couldn't let the opportunity pass you by
She's your one shining moment in over three decades
But you fear she's become bored with you
Tired of waiting
For your internal struggle to be over
Staying in your head
A hermit
You're about to let her get away
You are your biggest enemy
You have left you alone
You try not to think about your past
And you push through your present
Seeing happiness in the future
And your art is all you can honestly rely on

If it grows bored with you as everything and everyone else in your life has
You will cease to exist
Your coffee's grown cold in your life reflections
Get up and get a fresh cup
And just maybe you can break a cycle or two

The Night Shore

The moon hung low
Staring at the earth
And stirring the tide
The night called
A beckoning in the darkness
Skeletons of the deep
Long forgotten
Drifted upwards
Reassembling along the way
They reached the shore
Greeted by screams
The skeletons of the land
Covered their children's sockets
They noticed the clothes
Draping the bone figures
And looked down
Beyond the algae and seaweed
They were naked
And embarrassed
Those appalled shouted
So they turned
And returned to the watery depths

Chosen

You are chosen
To do great things
There's something deep within you
Something you haven't been ready to let out
Well
It's time
Pursue your dreams
Chase
What you have always been taught
Was unattainable
It's your time
It's your move
You were chosen for a reason
You can't hold yourself captive
Anymore
Let it out
Do it
What's stopping you?
Is it money?
Is it naysayers?
Is it too much of something?
Or a lack thereof?
Drown out the other voices
And listen to you
Listen to your heart beat
And your fluctuating breath
In
And out
In
And out
Now

Reach down
Deep inside of yourself
And find it
That thing you keep hidden
Pull it out
Perfect it
And show the world
Most importantly
Show yourself

Challenge Accepted

A new challenge sweeps across social media
We accept it
No it's not eating cleaning supplies
Or doing tasks blindfolded
It's simple
Being a good person
And helping the next
Let's see if this challenge catches on

2.0

Give away all your possessions
Cleanse yourself
And order more
Cut yourself off from friends
And family
And search for replacements online
Toss out your beliefs
And share someone else's
Don't speak to others
But like their posts
Change your name
Come up with something eye-catching
And controversial
Stop using your voice
Type faster
Using numbers instead of letters
Peel your skin off
Head to toe
And download more
If you're still you
You're doing it wrong

Hungry Friends

Clicks and chirps
They are loud and hungry
I'd feed them but they've had enough
This cave has gone frigid
Time to put another log on the fire
On occasion I'll throw them scraps
But they'll never have another meal like last night
My love decided she'd had enough
And was ready to leave
I couldn't let that happen
So I decided to feed my friends
Friends in need
Friends indeed
For they would never leave me
Nor forsake me
They grow hungrier still
If I wait too much longer
Between feedings
How much will my friendship mean to them?

Just the Way You Are

You like
You share
But you don't read
You work
You play
But you don't live
You nod
You smile
But you don't speak
You take
You give
But you don't love
You preach
You lecture
But you don't serve
You hate
You judge
But you don't see
You need
You want
But you don't change

Erotic Strangers

Our dreams were uploaded
Me on her
Her on me
We toss and turn
In our slumber bunks
Making love amongst the stars
We knew each other
Through sensual dreams
In reality
We eyed each other in passing
Like two starships in the night
We've never spoken
And probably never will
But I'll see her again
Tonight
And the next night
Strangers dreaming in unison

Rain Dance

Clouds bleed acid rain
The rain dance is interrupted
The villagers scatter
Their huts burn and melt down
Skeletons of men
Women and children scarred
They shield themselves but it's of no use
They cry out for a break in the storm
But it doesn't let up
It only rains harder
Lightning joins the fray
Igniting a flame-kissed land
The village burns
Be careful what you wish for

Masculine Love

The lights went out
Shades of black
Navy blues of the night pouring in
They felt for one another in the darkness
A rough masculinity of their secret passion
Lit their way
And they found each other
Somewhere in the middle
Between the hues of the moon
And the fire between them
Forbidden desire exploded
In a romantic rendezvous

SHADES OF YOU II

You're a seed, a cell
Tiny, insignificant
Floating around in a fishbowl of millions like you
Your surroundings, number of residents grow and shrink regularly
You're nameless as are your compatriots
Every once in a while there's an evacuation
Those you knew are never seen again
Only to be replaced by others of the same make
On the next release, you're caught in the current
In your new surroundings, you and the others find yourselves in a larger space
You swim
Magnetically drawn to something
A hub of sorts
An orb that you must be inside of
You don't know why but you keep going
The others and yourself aren't in competition
You don't understand competition
You don't know fight
You're just drawn to the orb
Pulled
It's shield feels thick as most of the others can't penetrate
The magnetism fuels your drive and you continue
You're through
The orb embraces you
You see others that had made it in
But the hub has rejected and they float lifeless
You don't know fear or worry
Nor curiosity for that matter
This orb has selected you to survive
Time passes

And it's the first time in your life that you're alone
A feeling you will understand later in life
You don't understand that you're being held
More time passes
You grow in ways you don't understand
A physical structure
Eventually you see what is becoming
You see your new hands from your new eyes
They move, you move them
Yet you still don't know what they are
Or what they're for
Your surroundings are getting smaller
And smaller as time passes
You feel a connection to the one who holds you
The orb feeds you, nurtures you
You're warm and its heartbeat soothes you
The hub stretches as you grow
You don't understand what's happening
You don't even think about it
You just are
The time comes
Another evacuation
You're not pulled out by a current
But the force of the hub pushing you out
Out of your comfort zone
Large hands pull you from your incubation
Your home
You see for the first time
Light
You cry and scream as you have no other forms of communication
You're separated from the hub
From the orb
And your new life begins
With no knowledge of what will come

And no regrets of what was before the lights
All you know is that you're new here
And you desperately want the feeling you had in the orb

Lost Room

Crooked days and bent nights
Narrow paths and narrower minds
They talk and talk
But never say anything
The walls close in
And the darkness swells
Their voices echo
Nonsense in shadows
Hysterics and panic
Binary in Morse Code
Questions unanswered
Dreams interpreted by children
They keep talking
We follow their voices
With limited space
Feeling our way
The walls are scarred
A calling in the distance
Audibly winding
Jagged corners
This room has ended
A door is found
Stop screaming

This is the End

The end is near
It's closer than you think
Close your eyes
Welcome to the brink
This is the end
I've loved you all I can
The end is nice
No questions to be answered
No comments to be made
No blinding lights
Cool darkness covers all
Golden silence
The music no longer speaks
And we no longer listen
This is the end
I've loved you all I can
No hurt
No pain
No sun
No rain
This is the end
I've loved you all I can
All that I can
With all that I am
All that I was

A Sad Truth

Suspected
Expected
Alienated
Imitated
Hunted
Black in America

Icy Home

Polar vortex
A winter blunderland
Ice cascades
Bitter cold
Outside and in
I can't feel the warmth of living anymore
Spiritual hibernation is required
Don't wake me
Until the sun returns

An Affordable Life

The taxes raise
Insurance unaffordable
Medicine's out of reach
The doctor's office is closed
Pockets are empty
Bank account collects digital dust
It's cheaper being dead

A Visitor

It was midnight
I was at my typewriter
When I heard a tapping
Followed by a harmony
I pulled my last sheet
And looked to the window
There she hovered
Backed by a starry sky
Air beneath her feet
And a song from her lips
My work was finished for the night
I invited her in
She licked her lips
Before singing in my ear
Her teeth sank into my neck
Her song flowed through my bloodstream
For that moment
We were one
Inspiration erupted
She left me with a curse
And I never saw her again

Lost Time

A crime he didn't commit
Plenty of time to think about what he hadn't done
People march in his honor
And picket for his release
He cries
He prays
He tries to survive
But he understands
The damage is done
A very visible stain on his life
One that won't wash clean with the truth

Derailed

You fell in love with me for the man I was
And I became the man you hated
I sincerely apologize
I'm trying to find my way back to him
So that you can find your way back to me
And we can be together again
The way we used to be

Voiceless

Loud clouds screech overhead
Larvae nibbling at your soles
The wind howls down empty corridors
You'd scream for help if your vocal cords still worked
Shadows race along the ground
You try to keep up
But the ground is unstable
Squish goes each step
Your nest egg hatches
A voice is found
How will you spend it?

Bugs

My skin melts
And freezes disproportionately
The temperatures scale from hellish heats
To a teeth-chattering tundra
My mind is fried
I'm spent
Blockage
Everything fights to escape me
But no one's allowed out
The bugs are crawling again
The itch is back
I try to scratch it but my hands won't listen
My sleep is medicated
An insomniac's dreams of relief
The pressure is mounting
I need a release
My internal clock chimes
And my inner voice screams
"Somebody help me!"
But the Calvary never arrives
I slip in my earbuds
So the bugs don't make it in
Soothing voices tell me horrible things
To slumber-inducing melodies
Waking nightmares and drifting dreams
I chase sleep but never catch it
My heart thumps erratically
Frantically searching for the beat
My breathing is an accordion
Played during a seizure
I'm melting again

An abstract depiction of myself
The earbuds crackle and pop
Through the static
I hear the commotion that is my brain
The electric hum of the soul resonates
I don't recognize my thoughts
My inner voice now a foreign tongue
I swat at the bugs
The voices stop
It's cold
The itching continues
My body and mind aren't cohesive
Barely compatible
I cocoon myself in the fabric of stress
The bugs never leave
The blockage stays
I want to recycle myself and start over
Backspace to the white

Always Tomorrow

I'm addicted
I do too much
I know I do
I can't stop
I've tried but I'm not strong enough
I promise myself I'll do less tomorrow
But tomorrow comes
And so does my craving
I want to quit
I want to be free
Somebody save me from this disease
Save me from my addictive nature

A Choice

It happens every day
A word is heard
An action is seen
A seed is planted
Doubt or inspiration
A surprise awaits
Will we act
Or will we flee
It's a choice we must all make

Destination

Snakes slither at me feet
Spiders above me in webs
I step lightly
And stay low
And leap
Dodging scorpions
And land mines
My destination is up ahead
Will I make it?
Dangers are abound
And distractions aplenty
I'll need to rely on my blinders
My improvisational skills
My drive and desire
To reach it
Never mind the bites and stings
They're not real
I keep moving
Almost there

My Poor Back

The dagger in my back is dull
It took time and energy to penetrate
I thought they were my friends
The handle of said dagger has many hands on it
When I needed support
I was cast away
I was shunned
Ignored and forgotten
I reached out
Looking for a friend
Alas
I am alone
And my poor back is full of holes

DRIVE

What are you doing?
You're better than this
You know it
What are you waiting for?
There's no such thing
As the perfect time
What do you want?
Figure it out
Time is running out
Assess
Change
Act
Go for it

SHADES OF YOU III

You're an old, old man
You've been married four or five times
Despite saying you'd never get married again
After the first fell through
You're alone again
You miss everyone you've lost
Even those that ruffled your feathers
Your art left you long ago
You've held onto enough to get by
Enough to let you breathe
Enough to keep your heart beating
You have room for regret
But you don't have it in you anymore
Your past is larger than your future
But if you keep holding on to everything, you'll never smile again
You want to smile
You want to laugh
Of all your potential regrets
You regret not doing so more often before now
You were so angry in your youth
Holding yourself back when your peers were enjoying life
And now you're too old to do so
You're in your final days
You reminisce on the smiles you'd seen
And the smiles you'd caused
You don't realize the smiles at the time
But you see them now in hindsight
The line you've been standing in is getting shorter
Thinning out
And now it's time to let go
Let go of all the anger, regret, and worries

It's time to be thankful of everything
Thankful for opportunities that you had
Regardless of the ones you squandered
Your finger has a permanent indention from all the various wedding rings
As the indention in your mind from what they all meant at the time
No
No reason to regret anything
It all happened
Decisions were made whether or not you were proud of them
Executive decisions
Like the one you have now
To let go or to not let go
You can live the rest of your life thinking about what was
Or you can try to smile and laugh while you can
All the women you've loved over time have long forgotten you
You've lost many friends
The ones still here are in similar situations as you
Your parents left long ago
Upon your mother's passing you felt the orb connection one last time
And the first since you were a small boy
Yet upon your father's death
You had no recollection of the time you spent in his vessel
Let alone the moving from one orb into another for incubation
Yes
It's sad that our memories only go back so far
And yours have been fading for years
Your breath shortens and it's time to rest
Your eyelids blink before they close in finality
Everything you've ever loved or cared about appears as a multi layered collage
The lights dim darker and darker
A contrast to the lights that blinded you upon entering this world

Alone again
You're at peace
No more regrets
Those who will remember you, will
And those who won't, won't
You loved all that you allowed yourself to
If there's another life down the line
Perhaps you'll allow yourself to reach out more
And stop holding back

HAUNTING

I dream of you
All too often
I love you
But you haunt me so
I want to see you again
But not against my will
What will you tell me?
What will you show me?
When you show up tonight
Will I let you in?
I don't want to
But I need to
The haunting never stops
And I'm not sure I want it to

POWERLESS

Stories spin in my head like a cyclone
I try to catch them but all I grasp
Are worries and memories
Regrets and remorse
Two hemispheres launch attacks on one another
My head pounds
Leave me be and let me work
Fingers to keys
Pen to paper
Paranoia strikes
An attack on myself
The guardrails are gone
And I've gotten off track
I try to find my way back
But I'm lost in my failures
My failure to provide
My failure to support
I feel powerless
I feel lost
And the stories are evading me
I give chase
But I'm bombarded
With my faults
My shortcomings
My absolute lack of power to fix the situation
I'm buried in the onslaught
Of myself

When I'm Gone

Death comes once in a lifetime
Accepting angels
Souls in a cosmic lost and found
What will become of me when I'm gone?
Will I live on through you?
Will you carry me with you?
When I'm gone
Will you remember?
I pray that you do
Or else
What has all this been for?

DEAD BATTERY

I try to start the ignition
But my battery is dead
My fuel has depleted
And my wheels are gone
I lay here motionless
Awaiting someone to tow me away

The Best of Us

For you
All of my love
I know you'll do great things
You were always the best of us
And your heart shows it
I am eternally grateful to have you
As we all are
Thank you, my love
For everything you are
And everything you do

MUSE

You are my muse
You've always been
You come to me
When I'm down
When I'm out
And you put the words through my fingers
You come to me
When the world has left me cold
When there's no one else but us
And you pull me out of the darkness with purpose
I'm in debt to you
When you leave you're still here
You'll never leave me
And I wish I could pay you back

Delivery of the Stars

Astronauts skydive to earth on the wings of angels
Caught in the palms of the masses
A rite of passage for innocent children
- and the guilty?
Not permitted at such services
The astronauts are carried on a wave
To the center of town
Where the spacemen deliver presents
Moon rocks to be used as fuel
They dance, they pray
They eat, they play
The stars await their curious intruders
The townspeople gather
The astronauts depart breaking the sky
A flash of light and they're gone
And the people watch the sky
Awaiting their return

FREE FORM

Good riddance to the flesh
Free from chains
Etherbound
Muscle aches
Stiff joints
Broken bones
Surgery after surgery
Patchworked and depreciated
Until I'm obsolete
Recycled
Born anew
With no shape
And no shame
Welcome free form thought
Gravity no longer applies
Lust not without form
Winds carry me
To open ears and open minds
And I live again
Through inspiration

Holding On and Letting Go

Tomorrow looks like yesterday
Another day soon forgotten
Today is mandatory
We must break through
To get to a future
We'll only remember in pieces
We don't get to pick the moments
And most will slip away from us
But we have them for a brief time
Hold on
And learn to let go when the time comes

REM NIGHTMARES

The electric brain pulses
Synapses sizzle and pop
Anxious nerves await calming
Notifications sound
Low battery alert
Power down and sleep it off
Tomorrow may be better
It may even be worse
But it won't be like now
Buzzing and beeping
The alarm sounds
Time to wake up

This Writer Will Self-Destruct

My greetings smell like my father's kisses
I've found an easy out
Sobriety is a harsh reality I've chosen to ignore
I don't want to come down
Don't want to be sober
I want to feel good while I self-destruct
Hospice care for myself
I'm falling down a dark spiral
And I can't get out
Then again
I've never really tried

Land First, Jump Second

The stone is thrown
The surface breaks
My heart ripples
The current shifts briefly
Suddenly
I gasp
The ripples widen
And eventually fade
The natural flow returns
My breathing steadies
Airflow
Heartbeat
Jump
Break
Ripple
Fade

To Whom It May Concern

This may be the last time
We ever speak
So I want to be very clear
I love you
I've always loved you
So when the world seems loveless
Remember, you have someone who cares
I'm proud to call you my friend
You're a wonderful person
And you aren't told enough
We've had our rough patches
Our head butting
But I've always respected you
And cared about you
We don't talk as often as we should
And we rarely see each other
But know that if this is the last time we speak
You're loved
You're respected
You're wonderful
And I would miss you
As I hope you would me
If this is it
Then I wish you a bright and fruitful future
And know
That I'll always be your friend

Growth

A three-legged dog hikes his nub
He waters the weeds breaking free from the concrete
The dog goes on a hunt for food
The urine bakes dry in the hot summer sun
The weeds grow at a steady pace
Stepped on
Urinated on
It grows still
Resilient

The Company We Keep

This lifeboat is worse than the wreck
Suspicious characters the lot of us
We watch but don't trust
Survivors in the night
Movement is little
We're sinking
Too much weight
Deliberation
I'm voted off
I swim beside but I can't keep up
I'm cast away
In the moonlight I see them
Sharks circling me
I can't make out how many
Six, seven
Three or four
My screams are ignored by my former party
The circle closes in on me
But they don't eat
They carry me past the lifeboat
And onward
The survivors watch
As my new party takes me into the moonlight
Know who to trust
It's not always who you think

Together Tomorrow

Believe in me
As I have you
Follow me
I will show you the way
If you want
If you wish to stay
Stay
Don't look back in regret
Now take my hand
And I'll take you
You'll be safe
And well-guarded
We'll rebuild
And live the best of lives

An Appointment in the Outer Realm

North of Heaven
South of hell
Choose a gait
Ring a belle
Waiting room for a millennium
Receptive receptionist
A water cooler conversation in the cosmos
What are you in for?
Coordinates are set
The vault opens
Mark I
Mark II
Set sail
The gods will see you now

Bitter and Sour

You're just a rock in my shoe
That's what I think of you
You hurt me with every step
It all goes south
When you open your mouth
You offend me with every breath
A thorn in my side
Just along for the ride
You bleed me with every cut
You're a splitting headache
And you think we're the same make
You taunt me with every strut
You take my breath away
And then beg me to stay
I'm sorry but I have to go
It's been real, it's been a trip
A hatred on automatic drip
Remember that I told you so

A Reflection

Yellowed crooked teeth
Smoke on the breath
Overweight for too long
Work too much
Never taken seriously
Love too hard
Never satisfied
Always looking for more
Beyond the horizon
Addicted and afflicted
Need more
But want less

These Hands

My mind is a wonderland
By my hands are too conservative
I try to paint the picture
But the words have set their footing
I need to break free
Bound
To these chains I've dressed myself with
I can't move freely
My mind has a wall around it
If I can just get over it
Perhaps I need to dig down
And go under
My mind is a zoo
That wishes to be set free
But the gatekeepers stay
Fear of rejection
Fear of failure
I dip my brush in the letters
And paint
I hate it
Too streamline
Too white bread
These damn hands
I need to sync
My mind is a carnival
But I'm not allowed on any of the rides
And I'm not allowed out
S.O.S.
I'd cut off my hands
Defeat my gatekeepers
But no picture would be painted

Frustration rising
When will I be free?

I Am the Darkness

I am not the flashlight
I am the darkness
You point and shine
But you never catch me
You never see me
Because you always see through me
I am all around you
I surround you
Yet
I can never be with you
I can't join you
Because you shove me away
You push through me
To catch a glimpse
I must not be anything
Worth seeing
Regardless
I am the darkness.

Here We Are

I am guilty
Everyone is guilty of something
But we're guilty of the same thing
They say the first step to recovery or resolving a problem is admittance
So if you're so inclined:
I,_____, plead guilty to the crimes against Mother Nature
To the polluting of our skies and the murder of our grounds
I am as much a culprit as the next in the defiling of Earth
She's raped
She's used and feels so
And us? We're the users
The rapists
But we can't point fingers, can we? We are all to blame
And we're just now worried of her deterioration?
The nerdy girl we picked on while she let us copy her homework, never thinking of her turmoil
The old man robbed and left for dead
Some of us claim to love her with bumper stickers on the backs of our pollution steeds
We cover her beautiful green figure with the grayest of concretes for runways on which such steeds ride
God made man
Man made commerce
Man made money in which we all strive for
We work to survive, but at a cost
In a kill or be killed situation, most of us kill the Earth while merely trying to survive
So is it really murder?
Perhaps manslaughter
Some unaware, clueless even

Some don't care at all
Others strive and make saving the planet their life's work...
Only to be brushed off as treehuggers, hippies, weirdos, wackjobs...even opportunists
Regardless, we're all guilty
And we will continue to be so
From the moment the first seed sprouted its first root, she spread her vines to say...
"Here I Am."
And then in we waltzed...
The bulldozers scraped the way for the parking lots to be paved and the concrete to be laid
And the chainsaws revved with hungry teeth as if we were to say...
"Here We Are."

She Doesn't...

She doesn't look at me like I want her to
She doesn't look at me like she used to
She doesn't look at me the way I look at her
She doesn't look at me anymore
She doesn't look at me
She doesn't
The fire in her has died down
Smoldering embers with a rare flame here or there
She's gotten cold
Her touch, once warm, now causes frostbite
Her heart is callused and there's nothing I can do to soften it
The sharp edge of romance has dulled
Its bluntness bruises instead of cutting clean through
The honeymoon long expected was a no-show
She deflects my compliments with a sneer and the coldest of shoulders
I don't excite her anymore
I'm not fun
My smile is extinguished
As is hers
She doesn't look at me like she'd looked at others in the past
She doesn't look at me as an equal
She doesn't look at me as a mate
She doesn't look at me with interest
She doesn't look at me
She doesn't
I'm yesterday's news
A memory sleeping beside her
A kiss goodnight is the farthest reaches
And it's a cold fleeting kiss
Chased

Maybe it's me
Maybe my light went out and left her in darkness
And she's stayed there
Maybe I did this to her
I can't help thinking that our love is dead
And I'm the murderer
She'd be happy with someone else
She'll look at them with passion
She'll look at them with a fire
She'll look at them with a smile
She'll love them the way she once loved me
She doesn't need me
She doesn't want me
It's clear
I'm taking up all her air
I'm wasting her time
I don't belong here
A mate grandfathered in
My presence isn't desired but accepted
I see mirages of her passion
But when I arrive it's long gone
She'll never look at me that way again
She'll never look at me the way she's looked at others
She'll never look at me again
She'll never see me
My heart's drying up
And discarded
As are my feelings for her
I express them and they fall on deaf ears
She should be with someone else
She can reignite her fire
She can smile
She can look at someone with interest
She won't be burdened with me

I'm her baggage
I'm convinced she regrets my not being lost in baggage claim
She pushes me away
And she doesn't pull me back

The Humanity Special

We answer questions with questions
And question answers we already know
Does all this make sense?
Would we agree if it did?
Are we really here to procreate and multiply?
Or was such a one-time pass that has been taken advantage of?
We spread quickly as an infestation of the highest intellect
Isn't that the fear we write about in science fiction stories?
We see everything in shapes
Dubbing our own and surrounding worlds as spheres
All the while placing our belief systems in boxes
And explain something natural like food groups with a triangle
We are our own therapists
Yet we're impatient and still expect to gain on our incredible fees
We all like to think of our time as full of purpose
And meaningful to most who know us
God's gift to the Earth
But sadly our essence plays out more like a fart in cosmic winds
Sometimes we feel like kings and queens atop of grand cliffs
With crisp eagle eye vision of the surrounding lands
And other times we feel more like a blind racecar driver
Every emotion and thought pattern is said to separate us from the animals
Could they feel the same but lack the voice to convey?
We want to save the earth
And use its resources
Have you ever heard of a parasite that wished to help its host?
Even going as far as rallying for and with other leeches?
Or protesting against them?
We want freedom
We don't like being told what to do

Yet we constantly strip each other of freedoms
And come up with new laws
New ways to tell each other what to do
The concept of time is man's
The only species that cares about and creates more deadlines is humanity
We set the boundaries for what time is
We spend it
We waste it
If we're not complaining about how fast time flies
Then we're complaining about how long it drags
Humanity's marriage is in a rut
We try but it's gotten stale
Just going through the motions
Life is a circle
We keep getting stuck in the grooves
The footprints and tire tracks from generations prior
The very same tracks and grooves are in our religions
Our politics
And what we consider family values
Courts and politicians will frequently highlight laws
Rules and regulations
Liberties and amendments
But leave the populous in the dark about those that will come back to haunt them
We base so much of what we do on what our long dead ancestors did
A cycle with very little change
A maze with just enough differences to keep you going
As well as keep you lost
We need to cut out the middle man
We need to learn our own national history and laws
Through personal exploration
If we wait for our knowledge to come from school, church, and the

government
We'll know exactly what they want us to know
Just enough to get by
Knowledge should be yearned for
Not looked at as a vitamin
Perhaps if it was sold as the cure for erectile dysfunction
Or an antidepressant
Knowledge would be more sought after
Perhaps we should start walking without following footprints
They won't tell you
And you'll be ashamed to voice it
But tradition is a prison
Humanity's pretty low on the totem pole
As far as the duration of our stay
We're nowhere near getting a promotion amidst the other species
But we constantly expect our vacation time, sick leave, and pay raises
Yet we don't act like humanity is a species unto ourselves
We segregate each other
By what turns us on or puts us off
I can't think of too many other species
That will willingly set up invisible cages to live in
And appoint rules at random like children on the playground
Making up games on the fly until a rule sticks
We live in the past
For the future
While waiting out the present
We don't know what we want
Even if we did we'd still question it
Humanity is constantly looking at the menu options for life
The line behind us is getting longer and we still haven't made a decision
Those on the other side are tapping their fingers on the counter
We want to order the Humanity Special

But what comes with such meals are subjective
We fight for survival all the time
Whether it's from ourselves
Or from the elements of the world
Illness and disasters
But maybe it's not as simple as we think
Maybe the universe is trying its damnedest
And we're just fighting extinction
Sometimes we eat the world
And sometimes the world eats us
Are we a boat with a hole?
Or are we the hole?
Are we keeping things together?
Or are we led to believe so while being kept together ourselves?
The cosmic rubber band
Stretched beyond its limits

An Alien in America

I don't know how I got here
This world, this time is strange
I haven't been here long
Not long enough to get to know the people
But long enough to get a feel for the fabric of society
I've read up and studied their history
The world, or America, the country I find myself in
Is an interesting melting pot of emotions
The people here are free
But instead of enjoying their freedom
They seem more intent on stripping others of theirs
Presumably to have more freedom for themselves
I'm sure they know what they're doing
Fascinating...
In conjunction with the word 'fair'
I'm hearing a lot of 'me' and 'I'
But no 'us' and 'we'
Everyone wants control
And no one's in charge
They speak a lot about their 'rights'
Specific terms of agreement for the freedom they argue over
The people make none of the decisions
And make all of the demands
It's an interesting push and pull
I would venture a guess that without such constant turmoil
Their society as a whole would crumble
So, in essence, they fight to thrive
Or perhaps it's insisted
By who or what, I'm not exactly sure
Perhaps...
They receive orders from the little devices they all carry

Even the little ones are issued with them
Very wise of their Gods
They seem to be quite taken with symbols
Most of them on rectangles of fabric
I'm assuming the sight of these acts as a trigger
Thus spawning the turmoil
Thus keeping the American Machine running
The cogs are all in place
Occasionally oiled when needed
There are inhabitants that love this world, this country
And there are those who are less enchanted
Regardless, they both take part in the machine's ignition
Even if they don't realize it
It's quite genius of this America, really
I applaud them
But it's time to get back home
I wish these strange people the best
Now if I can only find my way back...

Do You

I've fought for more
And worked for less
But I still try my best
Even when I'm at my most complacent
I try my best
All I can do to stay me
When accidentally becoming someone else
Is always a possibility

A Feast

A skipping heartbeat, a blood curdling scream, a clatter
I sprung from my coffin to see what was the matter
Once bright stars, the sharp moon, and the dead trees dancing all shrouded in dark matter
Cosmic fogs crept over the crypts and their tenants before reaching the lake
The bodies dug themselves out, instantly following the shimmering fog in their wake
The thick mist rested upon the dark water's surface and gave separation to the oils
Fish eating fish eating fish rose to the top, soon joined by every living thing pushed by the waves of water boils
I joined my neighbors to the shores of the midnight market where we stood and waited as pulpless rind
Unintelligible murmuring filled the air, thick and pungent, as the hours aligned
The land-bound clouds parted to the platter of death before us, a feast for those long hungry and starving for touch, and we dined

Short Honeymoon

Cigarette burns on my wife-beater
Ashtray on a broken speaker
Bloodstains on a wedding dress
First time for everything
When's dinner?
Where have you been?
My heart's cold, my beer's warm
Bottle's empty, this honeymoon's gotten old
I scream, I cry, I throw
But you're not around to take my abuse
My hand's have softened
The calluses left soon after you did
I'm falling apart
I loved you but the only way I knew how

Decisions, Decisions

We decide who decides and a concrete decision is never made
Choices are made to appease but it's never the choice we need
We choose our watchmen but then we watch them with suspicious eyes
The lesser of evils and we make our selection
Nothing makes sense, no rational thought
We lead by emotions but logic's taken a walk
We want it all but only when we want it
We don't like surprises if it's an inconvenience
We want love and adoration but we don't like being watched
We love but only in return
While we judge first
Shoot first and ask no questions
The answers are there like the elephant in the room we choose to ignore
Choices, it's all choices until our choice is whittled down and finally taken away
Our decisions are not our own
But mere doors to get out of the room we're locked in
And we hold the keys but we can't see them
We have to believe it but it's hard to swallow
Our beliefs appear strong but are thin
As shown when questions are asked and only stock answers are given

The Front Page

Corrupt cops
Biased media
Opinion regarded over fact
Watchful eyes all around
An open ear hears all
Far right
Far left
Extremists
Those in the middle
Casualties of war
Everybody's got a take
Vantage points distorted
Frequencies jammed
Static expressionism
Judgments made
Decisions overturned
Protesting the tide
The petitions are signed
A hunger strike is feasted upon
Gluttonous politicians fill up
And they're hungry again

The Reptile Bar

Textile reptiles
Drinking lager at the bar
The lizard orders two
One for it and one for its tail
The crocodile orders dinosaur crude ale
Pours some out for its ancestors
The snake coils around its glass
Flicking its tongue into the drink
The turtle returns to its shell
When it's had too much to drink
The frog orders with a side of flies
It's turned away
No amphibians allowed
The lizards call for more brew
And do shots off the turtle's shell
The snakes release their grip on their glass
And order another
Salamanders walk by and rethink entering
The crocodile conjures up old reptilian drinking songs
The bar breaks out into chorus
Drinks flow and the scaly be merry
The Reptile Bar is open 'til winter

The Dawn Limited

Night falls
And we catch it in our embrace
You hold the moon in your eyes
With the stars at your side
This night might be our last
But we'll spend it together
Dance with me
We shan't be able to again
Dine with me
The last supper
Love me as I have you
Tomorrow we shall be memories of strangers
Morning is on the rise
Goodnight and goodbye, my love
You hold dawn light in your eyes
With morning mist at your side
Morning comes
We slip away
And drift apart

ABUSED

You tell me you love me
But describe me as worthless
You tell me of my big heart
And describe me as selfish
You tell me you can't imagine life without me
Then you push me away
You tell me you trust me
But you question my every move
You tell me how wonderful I am
And focus on my faults
You tell me you pray for me
Then you damn me
You tell me you need me
Before asking me why I'm here
Well
Why am I here?

Bald Earth

Earthly pores sprout rooted follicles
Expansion over seasons
The ends of the roots far exceed the length to the top
The trunks are thick and covered in vines
Nurtured by nature
The natural ebb and flow of gas and liquid
Massages the soil's scalp
They grow in the wild
Manicured when they start to fray like nerve endings
Some reach their maximum strength, some nowhere close
Strength examination
They're severed at the base
Bare soil with follicles awaiting rebirth
Some stay stumps of what could have been
The trunks are cleaned and shaved down
Particles are used to various degrees
Information, communication, entertainment
Ultimately discarded in the end
Soil, gas, liquid, expansion, extraction, repeat
The roots eventually dry up
The follicles cease functioning
Barren landscape
Expansion denied
Pores are destitute
Bald Earth

Keep Searching

Continue to seek
Strive to find
The answers are out there
We must keep searching
Look behind the secrets
Behind the words spoken
Within the shadows
We mustn't listen to "them"
It's out there
And we shall find it
We will persevere
We will find the answers
Together

Old and Gray

Snow on the ground
Ice in my heart
I want to find the warmth I once had
But I don't know where to start
Growth is stunted
And maturity's low
I thought I was loved
But it wasn't so
Red over white
My love runs cold
I procrastinated my youth
And now I am old
What tomorrow brings is a mystery
I'm either on the brink of failure
Or about to make history
Silver linings are a plenty
But these eyes never see
I'm all alone in this
If this is my existence
I'm taking a knee
I've fought long enough
I'm tired no doubt
This life as we know it is cruel and unfair
I'm sitting this one out
The fire has died
And the love is gone
I dreamed of being a king
While I lived as a pawn
When will I be redeemed?
When will I be whole?
I've searched all my life

And gambled away my soul
My life appears cold
And will soon decay
I want either the treasure I've hunted
Or my years of trying back
Now that I'm old and gray

Distract Me

Due to unfortunate circumstances
I am alive and well
I wake and work
Distractions, distractions
Depression and anxiety are very real
You needn't believe in either for them to take hold
For they believe in you
I distract myself with goals I've set
Along with life's tangible problems
I cling to hope like a life raft
Is it enough?
Will it ever be enough?
My dreams haunt my waking hours
And I sleepwalk through life
I'd ask you to wake me
But why bother?
Autonomously autopilot
Distractions, distractions
Feed me distractions
I need to get out of my head
And run my life for real
Before I crash and burn
The end is in sight
I'm so close to the follow-through
Please distract me

Timid Termite

Nightmarish notions and deep fried potions
Alcoholic nights and nicotine spikes
Broken promises and missed opportunities
The smell of fear and failure
Welcome to life
Where the pleasure hurts
And the pain feels oh so good
Impossible obstacles and clueless oracles
The communication station is down
Gravitational forces pull the navigational horses
Round and round the sun the carriage circles
Welcome to life
Where the work isn't worth the rewards
And the vacation is one to escape

Fast and Slow

I think with my heart
And feel with my head
Crawl with my logic
And run with my emotions
Life is fast
Progress is slow
I see with my voice
And speak with my eyes
Dream with my hands
And work with my mind
Life is fast
Progress is slow

Apocalypse Morning

Harsh winds blow
A rainbow pixelates
The trees bend at the roots
The leaves freeze
And burst into flames
The sky changes color
The ground darkens
The air thickens
Snakes retreat into the earth
Birds fly low
Under burning bridges
None of this matters anymore
The world has changed
Since we last woke
A technicolor Armageddon
The world has ended
Since we last spoke
To the beautiful end
We pledge our allegiance
The clouds flicker
And flash with light
We lift our heads high
The moon falls to pieces
And the sun fizzles out
We join hands
In the colorful darkness
And sing songs
Nocturnal delights
Morning never comes again
The alarm clock has retired
Life has changed

Since the sky dried
Life has ended
Since the batteries died
A beautiful morning like any other
Was our last
What was it all for?
We're afraid to ask

From the Soil to the Stars

From the soil to the stars
And everything in between
You fill my world
You make me believe
I'm everything I wish to be
When the sun sets
And the moon looms
You're here for me
My shelter
My escape
The air that I breathe
The waters I wade
You love me unconditionally
You're ride-or-die
Your touch calms my jumpy nerves
Your voice slows my racing heart
You carry all my emotions
In the palm of your hand
I'm everything I wish to be
Because you make me believe
You fill this world and the next
And everywhere in between
From the soil to the stars

Just One More

Teeth are chattering
Hands are fidgeting
I know I quit
I know how hard it was
Just one more
I'm begging you
Just one more and then I'll quit for good

This is Our Home

The street lights are tye-dye
The stop signs are in braille
The railroad tracks are clear and always looks like we'll derail

The mayor is schizophrenic
The taxes go up and down
The garbage men would come every day if their wheels were still round

The streets are clean
The yards are cluttered
The diner served my toast black and my coffee buttered

The pets go to school
The kids train in the park
The curfew is early but the ice cream man only comes after dark

The banks are open all night
The thieves have no one to rob
The workplaces in town have all merged into one lone factory job

The skies are sunny and blue
The ground is mostly sterile
The park can be dangerous as the pigeons are all feral

The street lines are different shapes
The crosswalk is narrow
The fees are low but the taxi is a wheelbarrow

The houses are upside down
The garages are right side up

The gas stations still price gouge and only sell fuel by the cup

The people live in the valley
The bookies live on the hill
The people watch fishbowl races but only for the thrill

The house is on the left
The yard is on the right
The salesman always meets his quota but only comes out at night

The chairs are very comfortable
The floors massage your toes
The walls are all reflective and the ceilings are covered in bows

The kittens have all their litters
The bird in the cage chirps a tweet
The dogs all do the housework and the owners beg for a treat

The children are all swimming
The old men are all fishing
The fishermen catch their new offspring to grant their wives' wishing

The people count the shooting stars at night
The children run to catch them with nets
The parents think it's silly to attempt but they still place their bets

The clock in the center of town ticks and tocks
The church bells ring out
The plumbing in town is thick and water takes forever to come from the spout

The insects loiter around the bug zapper
The people never hear the zaps but still hear them roam

The zapper is useless as beneath it the spider has made her home

The town square is oval
The dance is in town square
The couples attend and dance to silence just to give it flair

The suits and ties are checkered
The polka dot dresses have frills
The neighbors all stay in contact with the help of digital quills

The lampposts are surrounded by mirrors
The streets stay lit
The phone booths are useless anymore but still they sit

The plants grow while unattended
The shrubbery looks like garnish
The town is so delectable as is and they never want it to tarnish

The sky eventually pours
The city hall sends their fax
The statement is issued and everyone pays their rain tax

The lots are empty
The unicycles have taken over the handicap parking
The meter maid is blind and the seeing-eye dog keeps barking

The unemployment office is out of business
The police and doctors work for free
The post office negotiates and the teachers charge a fee

The mailboxes are corroded
The phone is a tin can
The communication still never falters as everyone meets to tan

The fishing is seasonal
The hunting is year round
The guns have been outlawed but the ammo is still around

The children have water fights
The adults watch and laugh
The parents would play as well but this way cuts their bill in half

The town is a maze
The roads wind at an angle
The lawn is often combed and brushed because the grass is known to tangle

The pools stay empty
The tubs stay full
The water becomes too thick and then the cord is pulled

The tethered frogs won't hop
The leash won't fit the turtle
The farms are digital but the land is fertile

The currency has changed
The milk is now money
The costs have gone up and the bees negotiate honey

The children play house
The dolls have dresses and the teddy bears have buttons
The kids make so much food, their toys have become gluttons

The funeral is tomorrow
The wedding date is set
The town's people celebrate and enjoy all they can get

The dimensions have overlapped

The space is smaller between the classes
The people see each other more clearly but only with 3-D glasses

The schools are packed
The prisons are hollow
The real estate agents have more work but new rules to follow

The gardener plants the seeds
The adults feed the animals the plants that grew
The children would do the feeding but aren't allowed out of the zoo

The street signs are amplifiers
The music comes from the speakers
The names of the streets are muffled by the squeaking sound of sneakers

The ring fits the finger
The glove fits the hand
The beach is walled off because the tide fits the sand

The people are happy
The goodness is secured
The vaccines are thrown away because all the diseases are cured

The sidewalks all have meters
The signals are out of range
The people stay employed because the lamps take change

The cars are red
The tires are blue
The auto shops have flourished since the invention of glue

The crops grow fast
The food is plenty for meals

The corn now grows on trees in banana peels

The maze walls are intricate
The postman often gets lost
The mayor occasionally hands out maps but only at a cost

The walk-ins are welcome
The hospital is a palace
The patients are treated with love and never with malice

The chapels are full
The pews are filled
The powers of change are issued to every resident but only used if willed

The issues aren't many
The weapons are free thought
The hurdles aren't hard to jump as all the wars are internally fought

The polka dots are painted with stripes
The swirls are straightened out
The town is so quiet there isn't a need to shout

The air is solidly still
The wind behind it blows
The two clash and push one another until a new weather grows

The house plants are shampooed
The carpet is mowed
The elephants are released when the camels are towed

The animals are plastic
The toys have fur
The people think this is strange but don't want to cause a stir

The answers are questioned
The council's attempts are worn
The problems are made but the solutions are born

The maze is rich with confusion
The people don't point out a flaw
The citizens are all in this world together and there's no need for law

The town is weird
The people are crazy
The lifeforms here are different but they certainly aren't lazy

The lollipops are salty
The meals are sweet
The town has had to make do since the butcher shop ran out of meat

The bats fly in the daytime
The birds fly at night
The flamingos came out of the sewers and gave the carolers a fright

The people watch the sky change
The night is long & day is short
The moon and the sun have a lot to sort

The streets are translucent
The sun is a strobe light
The people still commute but the space is tight

The radio is dead
The television is still on
The people will enjoy their entertainment until it is gone

The walls are thick
The ceilings are brittle
The houses would stand but their foundations are too little

The cars drive backwards
The front windshields are blocked
The bicycle lane is closed off because that's where the birds have flocked

This maze is neverending
There's no point to grieve
This is our home now and we can never leave

I Just Want to Say...

It's an everyday struggle
I want to end it all so badly
But there's too much to do
Too much to accomplish
And the very thought
That I might miss out on something amazing
Keeps me here
Now it's time to put down the razor
Put down the pills
And get back to work

About the Author

Christopher Michael Carter currently resides in Missouri with his wife. He lives with Multiple Sclerosis and writes in an array of genres and styles. He's presently hard at work on his next project(s). Until then...

www.ingramcontent.com/pod-product-compliance
Lightning Source LLC
Chambersburg PA
CBHW052151110526
44591CB00012B/1939